LET'S
TALK
ABOUT
THE

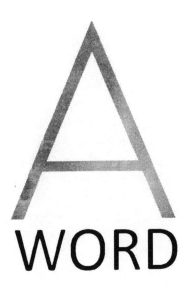

WORD

Shari Malcolm
sharimalcolm.com

LIBRARY OF CONGRESS CATALOGING-IN-PUBLICATION DATA
has been applied for.

Shari Malcolm
Let's Talk About The A Word
Edited by: Sadie Domineck
Published by: Saint Miles, LLC

ISBN: 173470281X
ISBN-13: 978-1734702811

Printed in the United States of America

CONTENTS

EVERY DAY I WAKE UP I INTENTIONALLY CHOOSE TO LIVE. EVERY DAY OF MY LIFE I FIGHT TO BE HERE WITH A SOUND MIND AND GOD'S PEACE.

And the peace of God, which transcends
all understanding, will guard your hearts
and minds in Christ Jesus

—PHILIPPIANS 4:7

"He will cover you with His feathers, and under his wings you will find refuge; his faithfulness will be your shield and rampart." — Psalm 91:4

Thank You.
May God Bless Each of You.
I am blessed to share this life with you.

Sharon and Ed My Amazing and Beloved Parents. Thank you for your unconditional love and friendship. You bless my life every day. It's an honor to be your daughter, and I'm praying I make you proud.

Mommy
You have been my rock , my best friend, my prayer partner and more than a mother -
We are spiritually and divinely connected. I thank God for you.

Thomas Lomack
I love you today and always.

Tari, Chelsea, Malcolm
You witnessed me fall, and you watched me get up —

I love you all so much, and I am blessed to be your mom.

My Aunts Sylvia and Frances

You are more than aunts and your love means the world to me.

Charlese Baby Sister

You did this. You planted the seed in my heart.

Belinda Finley

Girllllll, only us and God know what we have been through, but we fought and prayed together.
Wishing us a lifetime of friendship.

Amadi Leakes | My Spiritual Sister

Your prayers, encouragement and acts of kindness mean the world to me.

Kim Brown Cox

The day we met, I knew we would be friends. You are my prayer partner and my Mary.

Corey McKnight

When spirits connect…that is us. I thank God for sending me you.

Douglas Evans
I can always count on you.

Monique Hall
A true inspiration. Always full of advice and love.

Sadie Domineck
Thank you for seeing me. You are an Angel.

Enitan Bereola
Thank you for believing in me.

Confess your faults one to another, and pray for one another, that ye may be healed. The effectual fervent prayer of a righteous man availeth much. - James 5:16

I had to go through it

I had to walk through the fire

Every day felt like death but God kept me

I didn't get burned I didn't have one injury

God gave me beauty for ashes God kept my head up

When I couldn't move when I didn't want to live God kept me

The pain was so heavy calling your name was a mere

whisper

But God you heard my weak cry

Faith of a mustard seed

When I felt alone and spiritually abandoned God was there

I will forever praise your name

There's power in your name

Thank you God

I felt so weak so lost but you kept me

I had to walk through the fire

Every day I was smiling but my soul wanted to quit

But God you kept me

I don't look like what I have been through

I lost my mind and you blessed me with a new mind

God you are my everything

You kept me

1. MY BREAKING POINT

PAIN IS A STRANGE GIFT

Your purpose is hidden in your pain
Journal Entry Thursday, December 2, 2021

This is Day 2 of recovering from losing my mind. My husband is talking to me, but I'm not listening. As suggested by my mom, this is my first step at journaling. I've put them through so much.

I think it was Tuesday, yes it was Tuesday, November 30th in the evening and my life unraveled. I was eating a bowl of gumbo in the kitchen by myself and had an anxiety attack. An erupting warmth, and flooding hotness overcame my body. I wanted to run out the front door. And that's where it went downhill from there. Heart palpitations. I couldn't breathe. I cried in silence attempting to hide from my kids to throw up. My head was hurting. Normally I can breathe, pray my way out of it, look around and count the things I am grateful for. But I couldn't see nor speak. Faith felt fleeting, like it was in the distance slipping from me. It's the one thing in life that I hold and lean on the most - my faith in God.

My anxiety led way to a nervous breakdown where I couldn't find myself back to normalcy. My mind was pulling away from me. I was screaming and crying sitting on the floor on the side of my bed hoping and praying my kids would not see me like this. I needed help. Death was upon me; I felt it and was losing life fast. I was about to leave here; something was pulling on my soul and I was losing.

This was something I had never felt or experienced and I wasn't winning. Praying and praying and calling on God to help save me, I decided I would take my life and die. It felt like that was the only choice for it to stop. There was a spirit on me, and not the one I pray to. Something wanted me gone.

LET'S TALK ABOUT THE A WORD

ANXIETY

LOST. HOPELESS. SCARED. ABANDONED. CONFUSED. EXHAUSTED. ISOLATED. MOODY. IRRITABLE. DAZED. STUCK. PAINFUL. ALONE. PANIC. INSOMNIA. BREATHLESS. SUFFERING. INSECURE. DOUBTFUL. HEART RACING. PULSE ACCELERATED. TIRED. INCOHERENT. NON VERBAL. FEARFUL. ANGRY. DISAPPOINTED. HURT. NAUSEA. DIARRHEA. HEADACHE. VULNERABLE. DEPRESSED. NUMB. ANXIOUS. FRIGHTENED. SUICIDAL. TRAPPED. DEFEATED.

If any of these words describe how you feel, then you are in the right place.
Listen, please do not put this book down. No, I am not a physician, not a certified psychiatrist or therapist but I am someone who has suffered in silence with crippling and debilitating anxiety. Now, let me help you help yourself. You deserve this, and so much more.

As I am writing the pages of this book, I am fighting anxiety. I am right here with you; we are fighting together. You are not alone. You are not invisible. Your thoughts are valid. We will get through this together; day by day, step by step. God is a Healer. Each day I wake up I pray the heaviness of my thoughts are gone and each new day I remind myself that yesterday is in the past and today a new day begins. Do not hold yourself as a prisoner of the days that have passed. Clear your mind and start anew. Even with anxiety my life does not stop. I cannot sit still; my life keeps moving. I am taking the kids to school, staying on my daily routine pushing through the pain.

NOVEMBER 30, 2021

It happened. Today, I lost it. Full control over my mind was gone. Complete nervous breakdown. I unraveled and fell apart and for the first time in my life I could not put myself back together. There were no words. I could not talk, only moan. For the first time in my life I wanted to die. The pain was so bad and I had no control over my own body. I just wanted the pain to stop. I just wanted to go back to normal. But what was my normal? If I was honest with myself, I had been suffering in silence for a long time even convincing myself that I was fine. The only name I could call out was God. God help me. God save me. God, I do not want to die. God, you are a healer. God please heal me. God, please stop the pain. God, please stop my mind. God, please take over my body. God, make me whole again. God, please hear my cry. God hold me. God, I can't do this alone. God, please don't let me die.

I remember this day so clearly and play it over and over in my head because I am still trying to figure out how I got here?

I've had anxiety attacks before but this was different. For the next two months I had anxiety attacks all day every day. The pain was indescribable.

2. FINDING MY TRIBE

The first mistake with anxiety is isolating yourself from people that love you. When you isolate yourself you isolate your thoughts and that isolation leaves you stuck on a roller coaster of anxiety and the only person on the ride is you and no matter how hard you try to get off of that roller coaster you cannot get off by yourself.

The most important step to take when dealing with anxiety is to make sure you have a support system - your tribe. They know you have anxiety and they know what to do. In life, you have friends, relatives, associates then you have your tribe. They are hand selected by God; they are your angels. You can call on them for anything. They know your deepest thoughts, when you all talk it is always a safe and healing space. You are spiritually connected to your tribe.

My faith is the most important relationship in my life. Without God, I am nothing. There is no me.

Now, faith is the substance of things hoped for and the evidence of things not seen. - Hebrews 11:1

When you are alone and facing anxiety and you can't even find your way back to your normalcy back to a single moment of peace, call on God.

Back to November 30th - my husband was out of town. He drove to Florida to check on his 93 year old grandmother. His mom had passed earlier in the year and it was essential to check on granny. It was a regular day of doing laundry. It was getting dark and the kids were getting ready for bed. I remember sitting on the floor in my bedroom after having the first anxiety attack in the kitchen and this hot sensation flooded my body. My head was tight, my pulse was racing and my heart was beating rapidly. I could not think clearly. I could not even pick up the phone to call anyone. I could only call on God in my heart and in my mind. I stretched my arms in the air silently inviting God into my heart. Through uncontrollable tears I cried out for God. The words were so mumbled I could barely speak. My soul needed God. I needed help.

I started crying and could not stop gut wrenching tears. I needed this pain to stop. I felt like my brain had been invaded and it was no longer mine. By the grace of God, I called my mom.

I told her I needed her to listen to me. "I'm not well; I'm not myself. I'm losing it."

Then I called my daughters who were 13 and 14 at the time into my bedroom and told them how much I loved them and I told them I had failed them and I was sorry. Some have said I am mother of the year with all that I do for my kids even when I was a corporate executive and as a stay at home mom. I hugged and kissed my five-year old son and told him how much I loved him. Something was pulling at my spirit, something I had never felt before. It was a very clear and calm voice in my head. It was taking over me driving me to go into the kitchen and grab the pink butcher knife and stab myself in the chest. I had made the decision to take my life. It was the only way to stop the pain. I could not see the end or the outcome nor when the pain would stop. The pain was so heavy I felt burdened and I could not stop the heaviness of my thoughts. It was weighing me down. I was not myself and I could not function. I just wanted the pain to stop.

My mom called back and immediately began to pray over the phone with me. I remember hearing her tell the devil he could not have me and asking God to heal me. She told me to give my phone to my girls and made all of my kids cover me, hold me, hug me and lay on my back as I sat on the floor of my bedroom. I had vomited; I had diarrhea; I was weak; I was incoherent. All I could do was cry. Raising teenagers is not always easy to say the least and hugs and kisses become far and more distant. Having my kids hold me and hug me was everything my heart desired but at the time it was not even enough.

But God.

My mom and dad were on the way to our home; they lived 30 minutes away. I think they arrived in 15 minutes with my mom's driving. She stayed on the phone with me the entire time driving and praying.

I told her I wanted to bathe. She made my daughters stay in the bathroom with me while I showered. Normally showers are my refuge. The water is a place of peace for me. While I showered I felt so unattached to myself. I could not relax or calm down in the shower. My body was exhausted. I was mentally and physically drained. All I had strength for was rest. I could not gather my thoughts. I could not think. My mind was spinning and I could not slow it down. I felt like I had a heart beat in my throat as my pulse rapidly raced.

My husband was driving back from Florida swiftly driving on I-75 headed home. My parents had called him and told him I was not doing well at all and to get home as soon as possible. Get home. Get home. Get home. As soon as my parents arrived, my mom ran in my room, grabbed me, held me, touched me and prayed over me. The prayer my mom said still gives me chills. We didn't know what was going on but we knew the work that had to be done. We needed the words, the prayer and the pleading with God to heal me and save my life. The praise from her tongue with Hallelujah sounded different. They were coming from an unknown place.

My parents and the kids circled the bed and held hands calling out to God for a complete healing, pleading the blood of Jesus over me. My mom called her sisters on the phone and I remember my aunt telling me, "fight Shari; fight for your life." Slowly, and I mean slowly, the defeated thoughts of surrendering to death that so quickly flooded my mind begin to leave. It felt like an outer body experience. As I lay in the bed surrounded by my loved ones in tears I was flooded with questions. What had just happened? Was my spirit under attack? Was this spiritual warfare? Did I just lose my mind? A nervous breakdown?

It was anxiety.

3. LEARNING TO BREATHE AGAIN

Let me tell you how I got here. Have you ever heard the phrase, "Just sweep it under the rug." Instead of picking up that rug and shaking it to sweep up all the trash, you decide to politely cover the funk with the rug and not deal with the trash you overlook to walk over. Well, that is how I was processing stress – just sweep it, put it away, don't deal and come back to it.

I was compressing so much in my life and not dealing with it in the present moment and mostly because I am extremely non confrontational and some people just won't allow you to have a nice come to Jesus conversation. I am a great communicator for everyone else, but when it came to taking up space for Shari, I was on mute. I put everyone before myself. Everyone's feelings were valid except mine. Always putting myself last. I did not give myself the grace to relax, to recover and to release what I was holding on to each day. I did not create that safe space for myself that I created for everyone else. I listened and solved everyone's problems; pouring my all into everyone. But who was pouring into me?

My youngest daughter and I were invited to Houston, Texas for one of her best friends' 13th birthday party. Her family had recently relocated to Texas and her mom, whom I love and adore, had invited a few of her daughter's friends along with their moms. It was sure to be a good time, but I don't do well on airplanes...anxiety. Quite contrary though I have always loved flying. I could sleep through any flight. Not until recently did I become so overwhelmed being on a plane. I felt trapped and closed in with nowhere to go.

A month before the Houston trip, a few of my college girlfriends told me we were going to Miami and they were not taking no for an answer. "Just get your plane ticket and the rest is on us." But truthfully I did not want to go but I felt like I had to because they are so used to the loud and funny Shari, the spontaneous Shari that loves to have a good time and make everyone around her feel good.

Oh no, but wait - not me, not at this stage of my life being impulsive. Who's going to pick up the kids from school? I've got laundry and dishes waiting on me and Miami is not on my agenda for a Friday through Monday getaway. Anxiety... it always knows when to peak its nose in your business. Yesssssssssssssss, I wanted to get away from my husband and kids.
Yasssssssssssssssssssss I wanted to fly to the 305 and enjoy sitting in the end zone watching the Atlanta Falcons beat the Miami Dolphins, but anxiety will have you doubting your existence, let alone having fun and traveling. Who do I think I am?

I had anxiety when I said yes to the trip. I had anxiety when my husband said you deserve to go and have a great time. I had anxiety when my parents said they would keep the kids. I was anxious when I boarded that plane. I had anxiety sleeping in that beautiful waterfront downtown Miami property. I jumped up out of my sleep wanting to just run away, escape. I had anxiety inside the Hard Rock Stadium. I had anxiety traveling back home to Atlanta. And I suffered in silence as no one even knew. Not even through my smile and laughter, or through my joy and excitement, the people closest to me did not detect anxiety.

The second week of November, my daughter and I traveled to Houston, Texas. I tried to contain my anxiety on that plane so I could be excited, loving, and supportive of my daughter's first flight. I placed my cold water bottle under my neck as we sat on the second to last row of the Delta plane and prepared for takeoff. Houston, we have a problem! I had anxiety the entire flight. There were moments where I would exhale, it would be gone, and then boom - it was back within seconds!

I had anxiety at the guesthouse where me and another mom stayed. I felt it was necessary to be vulnerable and open and let the Mom know I was having an anxiety attack. I will never forget her words, "Anxiety, isn't that something you can control?" I remember screaming in my sleep and almost running out the front door. I had anxiety at Top Golf. I had anxiety at the birthday party. I had anxiety at the brunch. There were moments when I would feel amazing, I would feel myself laughing and talking, then inside of my head the anxiety would peek and make me feel defeated. No one can see the anxiety whispering in my ear. I just kept enjoying the party, but the anxiousness battling in my head left me mentally exhausted.

"Do not be anxious about anything, but in everything, by prayer and petition, with thanksgiving, present your requests to God. And the peace of God, which transcends all understanding, will guard your hearts and your minds in Christ Jesus" Philippians 4: 6 - 7

If it wasn't for the Lord, where would I be? Faith is the number one thing in my life. How can a person of faith have anxiety? How can a person who prays daily and talks to God constantly have worry or doubt? How could this be possible if you have faith? You can be a person of faith and deal with any and every emotion thrown to you in life. Your faith will bring you out of the darkest, scariest situations.

Anxiety will have you thinking you cannot have a quality of life. You have a good day, then anxiety will let you know tomorrow you will suffer. You control your thoughts, your thoughts do not control you. Simple statement and true.

INTERLUDE

HEALING SCRIPTURES

STAYING IN THE WORD RESTORES MY SOUL

Keep these healing scriptures close to your heart:

I can do all things through Christ which strengthens me.
Philippians 4:13
Affirmation: God with you all things are possible.

Do not be anxious about anything, but in everything, by prayer and petition, with thanksgiving, present your requests to God. And the peace of God, which transcends all understanding, will guard your hearts and your minds in Christ Jesus.
Philippians 4: 6-7
Affirmation: God I lay myself at your feet. Take away any anxiety God. It is not of you or your Word.

So do not fear, for I am with you; do not be dismayed, for I am your God. I will strengthen you and help you; I will uphold you with my righteous right hand.
Isaiah 41:10

Affirmation: God bless me with your strength and your desires for my life. Remove any fear from my heart. Take me from fearful to fearless.

The steadfast love of the Lord never ceases; his mercies never come to an end; they are new every morning; great is your faithfulness.
Lamentations 3:22-23
Affirmation: Thank you God for your new mercies. Keep my heart full of your love, grace and mercy.

Be strong and courageous. Do not be afraid or terrified because of them, for the Lord your God goes with you; he will never leave nor forsake you.
Deuteronomy 31:6
Affirmation: I am God's child. I am never alone. God is with me. I am strong. I am fearless. I will walk in His word. Cover me with your grace. God be the light under my feet. Go before me God and make a way. Guide me through troubled waters.

He put a new song in my mouth, a hymn of praise to our God.
Many will see and fear the Lord and put their trust in him.
Psalm 40:3
Affirmation: I will praise his holy and divine name all the days of my life. I trust you Lord.

Give your burdens to the Lord, and he will take care of you.
Psalm 55:22
Affirmation: God you are everything I need. My peace is found in you.

You were taught, with regard to your former way of life, to put off your old self, which is being corrupted by its deceitful desires; to be made new in the attitude of your minds; and to put on the new self, created to be like God in true righteousness and holiness.
Ephesians 4:22-24
Affirmation: Thank you God for making me anew. Keep me different God. Let my light shine for the glory of you.

I took my troubles to the Lord; I cried out to Him and he answered my prayer.
Psalm 120:1
Affirmation: My help cometh from the Lord.

He put a new song in my mouth, a hymn of praise to our God.
Many will see and fear the Lord and put their trust in him.
Psalm 40:3
Affirmation: God I praise your holy and divine name.

Now unto him that is able to do exceeding abundantly above all that we ask or think, according to the power that worketh in us.
Ephesians 3:20
Affirmation: God you are limitless. All things are possible when I put my trust and faith in you.

Rejoice in hope,
be patient in tribulation, be constant in prayer.
Romans 12:12

Affirmation: God thank you for being my hope and peace. God keep me in a posture of prayer.

So do not fear, for I am with you; do not be dismayed, for I am your God. I will strengthen you and help you; I will uphold you with my righteous right hand.
Isaiah 41:10

Affirmation: On my darkest days give me light. Bless me with the patience I need to make it another day.

Trust in the Lord with all your heart, and lean not on your own understanding; in all your ways acknowledge Him, and He shall direct your paths.
Proverbs 3: 5-6

Affirmation: No more of me God, all of you. Guide my words guide my heart.

And he said to them all, if any man will come after me, let him deny himself, and take up his cross daily, and follow me. For whosoever will save his life shall lose it but whosoever will lose his life for my sake, the same shall save it.

Luke 9: 23 – 24
Affirmation: God I surrender to you.

And he said to them, "Why are you afraid, O you of little faith?" Then he rose and rebuked the winds and the sea, and there was a great calm.
Matthew 8:26
Affirmation: Stop overthinking. You are made of greatness. Walk in your faith.

The Lord is on my side; I will not fear. What can man do to me?
Psalm 118:6
Affirmation: I will not be afraid of tomorrow. Only God has seen the future.

Blessed be the God and Father of our Lord Jesus Christ, the Father of mercies and God of all comfort, who comforts us in all our affliction, so that we may be able to comfort those who are in any affliction, with the comfort with which we ourselves are comforted.
Corinthians 1:3-4
Affirmation: God wrap your holy arms around me and bring me comfort. Stay with me Holy God.

I will instruct thee and teach thee in the way which thou shalt go: I will guide thee with mine eye.
Psalm 32:8
Affirmation: God guide my words and my heart. I trust you God.

Many are saying of me, "God will not deliver him." But you, Lord, are a shield around me, my glory, the One who lifts my head high. I call out to the Lord, and He answers me from his holy mountain. I lie down and sleep; I wake again, because the Lord sustains me. I will not fear though tens of thousands assail me on every side.
Psalm 3:2-6
Affirmation: No matter the pain in the world I stand with you God. Be my fortress of strength.

When the righteous cry for help, the Lord hears, and rescues them from all their troubles. The Lord is near to the brokenhearted, and saves the crushed in spirit.
Psalm 34:17-18

Affirmation: I lay my burdens at your feet God, have your way.

Don't rejoice when I fall my enemy: because when I fall, I shall arise.
Micah 7:8
Affirmation: Prophesy over my life God better days are ahead.

What, then, shall we say in response to these things? If God is for us, who can be against us.
Romans 8:31
Affirmation: God thank you for covering me protecting me with your goodness I trust you God.

When I am afraid, I put my trust in you.
Psalm 56:3
Affirmation: When I am surrounded in darkness God carry me through to the light. You have never failed me God.

The Lord is my strength and my defense; he has become my salvation. He is my God, and I will praise him, my father's God, and I will exalt him.
Exodus 15:2

Affirmation: God I will praise you all the days of my life. Hallelujah! Glory to God!

I pray that out of his glorious riches he may strengthen you with power through His spirit in your inner being.
Ephesians 3:16
Affirmation: God I trust the lesson plans you have for my life. Have your way God in my life.

God's power works best in our weaknesses.
2 Corinthians 12:9
Affirmation: God make a way for me even when I can't see the next steps walk with me God

Therefore, if anyone is in Christ, the new creation has come: The old has gone, the new is here.
2 Corinthians 5:17
Affirmation: God make me of you. Remove anyone or anything from around me that is not of you. Guide my words and my heart.

I lift up my eyes to the mountains where does my help come from? My help comes from the Lord, the Maker of heaven and earth.

Psalm 121: 1-2

Affirmation: God you are Jehovah Jireh. I am blessed and grateful. I have everything I need. You created me and there is purpose in my life. Thank you God.

Find Your Light,

Find Your Joy,

Find What Makes Your

Soul Happy

HEAL
BECOME SOUND OR HEALTHY AGAIN.
ALLEVIATE A PERSON'S DISTRESS OR ANGUISH.

4. DARK NIGHT OF THE SOUL

GOD HELP ME

I couldn't talk; I was non-verbal. I could not eat; I had a loss of appetite. I could not move and my body felt so heavy. I could not sleep; my eyes would not shut. I could not focus; my heart and pulse were racing so fast. All I could do was call on the Lord. God Help Me. God Help Me. I am hurting; please help me. Please save my life. I do not want to die. The pain was so bad; I felt like I was having a nervous breakdown. I just wanted the pain to stop and death felt like the only way BUT GOD. God is a HEALER. HE heard my Cry.

YOU'RE NOT ALONE

Anxiety will have you feeling embarrassed and ashamed and as if you are the only one on earth going through this. Well I am here to tell you,

you are not alone. Millions of people are experiencing the exact same anxiety you are experiencing. Do not be afraid to tell your story and share your truth to find healing. According to ADAA, an estimated 264 million people worldwide have an anxiety disorder. Five women are nearly twice as likely as men to be diagnosed with an anxiety disorder in their lifetime.

FINDING YOUR WAY BACK TO NORMAL

I just want my brain to relax. I just want to be and feel normal again. Better than normal. Excited again to LIVE. Excited to start a NEW day. Excited to just be.

PTSD (Post Traumatic Stress Disorder)

After days and months of anxiety attacks, you wake up embracing, waiting for the hit…waiting to feel the anxiety again. It's like anticipating a tornado. I begin to document the anxiety attacks. I begin to take notice of any and all triggers. Was it stress related? I removed all caffeine from my diet and begin to be extremely intentional about my day to day routine.

DETOX MY MIND

Controlling and decompressing my thoughts to calm my mind from overthinking is always the goal. One of the first things I did to detox was unplug from all social media and downloaded an app Calm on my phone and used Youtube to play ocean music and nature sounds. Because I had so many anxiety attacks every day for three months, I was EXHAUSTED and my memory was failing me. To help with my memory, my mom encouraged me to download her favorite game Candy Crush, which I played for a few days, but I enjoyed the word games much better. I began to play every day to build up my muscle memory, and it worked. My husband and I both started staying up until the a.m. hours playing.

I started my day in prayer, read scriptures daily that fed my spirit, listened to my gospel playlist, made myself a cup of herbal tea every day, fed my mind positive thoughts, imagined the future I wanted for myself and family, stayed in a place of gratitude, talked to God all day, developed a positive routine that fed my mind positively and spiritual thoughts constantly. And I begin to walk outside around the community lake every morning after taking the kids to school. Listening to my gospel music, talking to God while the Sun warmed my soul. This gave me peace.

Being a mom of three and a wife, I always felt the need to be on the go all of the time. I would take the kids to school, come back home and immediately start to clean the house, laundry and fit in a grocery store run. I was the Room mom at my kids school which meant I was responsible for being present for any activities in the classroom as I was needed, met for an occasional breakfast or lunch with the husband and ran most of the errands but never accepted space for myself to simply relax. I always felt guilty for thinking about going back to bed or taking a nap, curling up with a book or just laying on the sofa watching television. Why is that? Why would I feel guilty for relaxing? I have worked all of my life in Corporate America and I don't think I got comfortable being at home. I felt like I had no purpose. I did not want my husband to come home and see me relaxing or lying. in bed. Why is that? Why was I so afraid of what other people thought? After working in Hospital Administration for 15 years I knew it was time for a change. The environment, the people, it was so stressful. The work hours, the distance from home, I missed my daughter's school programs. There was never enough time in the day to spend with my family, love on my babies after working all day. I resigned with my husband's support and join the film industry working in accounting and payroll. I loved it. I loved the environment, the people, meeting the celebrities and definitely craft services. The industry fit me well but the grueling hours did not fit my family lifestyle. Wrapping up my last movie, I was so happy to spend the Summer with my daughters and return to set in August; however, we found out we were expecting and it was a boy right on time for my 40th birthday. When my Son was born, I became a stay at home Mom. I did not want to miss one second of his life. It was a blessing to be home with him every day and with my daughters. My Son was diagnosed with Autism at the age of three years old and I had the time to take him to every doctor's appointment. I was present.

But I could not understand my assignment – which was likely the reason I could not relax as I was constantly processing data that led to anxiety. I was grateful to be home but I did not have my own income and deep down inside that bothered me. I was constantly searching for my purpose that I equated with having money.

I was perpetually seeking; looking for something to do. What was I running from? I always felt guilty for not working and contributing financially to the household.. But what God revealed to me was that I AM WORKING. I am taking care of my family (my biggest assignment yet) and my husband and I have a partnership. He is able to work and provide for our family because I am taking care of home and kids. That was the balance I was missing to understand my purpose.

After three months of consistent depression, anxiety and pain, I've got it!! We must take the time for ourselves. More visits to the spa and bath houses, mornings and afternoons of relaxing in the bed, binge watching a show by myself, not feeling guilty if I am taking the day to relax, more stops at the bookstore with a cup of hot tea, long walks at the park around the lake and doing what makes Shari satisfied. I stopped caring and worrying what anyone would think about me. I had to detox my mind of past thinking and make myself a priority. I created my day the way I desired and watched God give me my life back. The hardest thing I have ever had to do was fight for myself. Fight every single day for my mind back, praying profusely to God to heal my mind. Showing up for myself every day and proving to God that I am worthy to be here. I want to be here God. I choose to live God. Show me your plans for my life God.

RESET
SET AGAIN OR DIFFERENTLY

5. PRAYER AS A LIFELINE

Journal Entry Monday, December 6, 2021 – I'm taking it one day at a time and slowly getting back to me, actually a new me better than before. I am praying and healing. Trusting God through the process.

A prayer for those dealing with the A word
Just hold on, don't give up!
God, I can feel You. I feel Your presence. Carry me, God; be my strength. I trust you, God. I shall not want. God, you provide all of my needs. I lift my hands to thee; I praise your Holy Divine Name. Thank you God for your peace, protection and covering. My cup runneth over and I shall not want. You provide me with everything I need. Your goodness, grace, mercy, forgiveness and redemption – Glory to God. I feel you, God. I seek your truth, God. Wrap your arms around me, hold me God.

God you are a healer. Glory Hallelujah! I cast all my anxiety to you.
Amen

Self Care Plan
45 Things You Can Do Today to Reduce Anxiety

1. Create a mental and physical space that feels good to you
2. Dwell in your happiness and peace
3. Create healthy boundaries for yourself to decompress daily and live in the moment
4. Accept the things you cannot change, not worrying about tomorrow
5. Practice deep breathing, meditate and pray
6. Master the art of saying no
7. Focus on yourself
8. Prioritize your day
9. Sleep to feed your soul
10. Find your supportive friend tribe
11. Fill your empty thoughts with productivity
12. Create your self-care music playlist
13. Learn to relax
14. Live a life of agape love
15. Dance

16. Remove toxicity from your life
17. Forgive
18. Laugh
19. Relax
20. Say no to procrastinating
21. Conquer your goals
22. Rediscover your relationship with God
23. Find your light
24. Enjoy life
25. Start a hobby
26. Detox from social media
27. Imagine the best version of yourself and go for it
28. Dream
29. Be conscious of the food you eat give God all of your worries and troubles
30. Turn your pain into purpose
31. Clean out your friend circle
32. Get out of your own head
33. Create healthy boundaries
34. Start therapy
35. Develop a mindset of gratitude
36. Seek the sunlight
37. Get active
38. Start walking and exercising
39. Invest in vitamin supplements
40. Stay hydrated

41. Speak positive affirmations over your life
42. Love on yourself
43. Take the first step towards your destiny
44. Create a night time routine to ease your mind before bedtime
45. Allow yourself to be properly loved

Take your life back.

THE POWER OF YOUR MIND

Mind over matter is what my mom would say to me all the time when I was feeling stuck mentally. And it is true – mind over matter. God does not give us the spirit of fear but of power, love, and a sound mind. Anxiety and panic does not come from God, but it is all in our minds. It used to be so hard for me to say that because I always wanted to place this horrendous blame of anxiety on someone or something other than myself. But it is true…it's all in your mind.

FAITH

I recently came across a video on YouTube with a gentleman named Salt Strong and I had an epiphany. It mentioned faith, and yes we have faith in God, but do you have faith in yourself? This deep question requires deep thought, and when I thought about it, I didn't have faith in myself. I have so much in God but none in myself. When I reflected on my life, I wondered where my faith in myself was. I can believe in everyone, lift and encourage those around me, but not myself. I was always the co-pilot, trusting someone less qualified than me to be the pilot, not realizing God has blessed me to be super talented and gifted if only I believed.. Where has my faith in myself gone or did I ever have it? Why do I doubt myself and my God given gifts? As I continue to reflect and grow, I have learned to "sit in it". Sit in my thoughts, sit in my pain, sit in what is confusing or bothering my spirit and listen to the Holy Spirit speak to me. In these moments of prayer and meditation I found the most clarity, truthfulness and understanding about myself. Taking the time to reflect on situations in my life has allowed me to grow as a human and move forward with grace. I am no longer carrying the heaviness of my thoughts or drowning in guilt or blame to others. Every lesson in life is for me even if I was not at fault. There is always a lesson to be learned; it helps you mature and grow. God's lesson plans are everywhere.

Add this to your prayer: God bless me with faith in myself. Change my mindset and encourage me to speak positive affirmations over myself.

6. COMMUNITY CARE

TRIBE LIFE

You will not suffer in silence.

Who's in your tribe? It is equally necessary and imperative to have family, friends, or strangers that will pray for you even when you can't pray for yourself. Gather a tribe that you trust, knows you and accepts your vulnerability without judgment or condemnation . Find your tribe that you can call or text at any time of the day when you need help. You are not alone.

INTERLUDE

SELFIRMATIONS

I AM LOVED
I AM NOT ALONE
I AM WORTHY
I AM ALIVE
I HAVE PURPOSE
I AM A BELIEVER
HALLELUJAH
I AM WELL
I AM ABLE
I AM STRONG
I AM CALM
I AM RESILIENT
I AM A DESIGNER'S ORIGINAL I AM
COURAGEOUS

I AM FEARFULLY AND WONDERFULLY MADE

I FEAR NO EVIL

I CAN DO ALL THINGS THROUGH CHRIST
WHO STRENGTHENS ME

I AM CLOTHED WITH STRENGTH AND
DIGNITY

I WANT TO LIVE

I DESIRE THE BEST LIFE FOR MYSELF
I AM CHOSEN
I AM A CONQUEROR
I AM VICTORIOUS
I AM GOD'S MASTERPIECE
I AM DOING MY BEST
I HAVE HOPE I HAVE FAITH

I HAVE A FUTURE
I AM A CHILD OF GOD
I AM ENOUGH
I HAVE FAITH IN MYSELF I AM WORTHY
I AM BOLD
I AM BRAVE
I AM A FIGHTER
I AM A SURVIVOR
I AM FREE OF WORRY AND ANXIETY
I AM GRATEFUL
I BELIEVE IN MYSELF
I LOVE MYSELF
I CHOOSE TO BE HAPPY
I DESERVE TO BE HAPPY
I SEEK HAPPINESS
I AM AT PEACE
I HAVE A POSITIVE ATTITUDE

I AM BECOMING THE BEST VERSION OF
MYSELF

I HAVE PASSION IN MY LIFE

I DESERVE TO BE HAPPY
I HAVE OVERCOME MY FEARS
I CAN CONTROL MY THOUGHTS
I RELEASE ALL ANXIETY FROM MY MIND AND
BODY

I PLEAD THE BLOOD OF JESUS OVER MY
LIFE

I REBUKE ANXIETY FEAR DOUBT PANIC
WORRY

7. WARSHIP

I was in a battle. This was a fight for my life. Even if you don't know the enemy or understand the attack, you must be prepared for war. Always remember God is your friend and he will not fail you. I was in spiritual isolation with no social media, socializing and no "hey girl"l hey phone conversations. God clothed me for battle and prepared my heart through worship music and the Word of God.

The only people that I communicated with other than my husband and children were my family and prayer warriors – altogether less than 10 people. When you are in the midst of an attack, you cannot always pray for yourself. Sometimes you cannot find the words, but God knows your heart. Surround yourself with prayer warriors. Every day, I filled my spirit with gospel music, scriptures, daily prayers and inspirational sermons. This equipped me for the battle ahead and it worked. I had lost my desire to speak and sing. Find your voice again through music.

I offer you my Gospel playlist that stays on repeat in my house filling every room, including the shower:

Song and Artist(s)

Track 1: "Manifest" Johnathan Nelson

Track 2: "Your Destiny" Kevin LeVar & One Sound

Track 3: "Take It to the Lord in Prayer" Nolan Willilams, Jr.

Track 4: "He's Preparing Me" Daryl Coley

Track 5: "Deliver Me (This Is My Exodus)" Donald Lawrence and the Tri-CitySingers featuring Le'Andria Johnson

Track 6: "Better Days" Le'Andria Johnson

Track 7: "Life and Favor" John P. Kee

Track 8: "Nobody Greater" Vashawn Mitchell

Track 9: "For Every Mountain" Kurt Carr Singers

Track 10: "Total Praise" Richard Smallwood

Track 11: "God Favored Me" Hezekiah Walker

Track 12: "You Know My Name" Tasha Cobbs Leonard

Track 13: "Help Me" Tamela Mann

Track 14: "Thank You So Much" Earnest Pugh

Track 15: "Jehovah Jireh" Jekalyn Carr

Track 16: "Hymn of Breakthrough" Israel Houghton

Track 17: "You're Bigger" Jekalyn Carr

Track 18: "I Smile" Kirk Franklin

Track 19: "Latter Rain" Men of Standard, Kirk Franklin God Take Care of Me Men of Standard

Track 20: "Well Done" Detrick Haddon

Track 21: "Grace" Charles Jenkins & Fellowship Chicago

Track 22: "Hold On" James Fortune & Fiya Featuring Monica and Fred Hammond

Track 23: "Jesus is Love" Commodores

Track 24: "Cast Your Cares" Donald Lawrence & The Tri-City Singers

Track 25: "Go Get Your Life Back" Donald Lawrence & The Tri-City Singers

Track 26: "He Rebuked the Red Sea" Donald Lawrence & The Tri City Singers Featuring Sheri Jones Moffett and Kristen Lowe

Track 27: "Grace" Jonathan McReynolds

Track 28: "Million Little Miracles" Elevation Worship

Track 29: "Shall Not Want" Elevation Worship
Track 30: "HER" Isaac Carree

Track 31: "Order My Steps In Your Word" Al Hobbs & GMWA Women of Worship

Track 32: "Mary Did You Know" Maverick City Music

Track 33: "Never Let Me Down" James Fortune

Track 34: "You're the Lifter Ricky Dillard Featuring Tamela Mann

Track 35: "For My Good" Todd Galberth

Track 36: "He Did IT" Evvie McKinney

Track 37: "Jireh" Maverick City Music Featuring Chandler Moore, Naomi Raine

Track 38: "More Than Anything" Lamar Campbell & Spirit of Praise

Track 39: "I Trust You" James Fortune and FIYA

Track 40: "Love Theory" Kirk Franklin

ANEW

In a new or different, and typically more positive way

8. PURPOSE RISING FROM PAIN

WHAT GOD HAS FOR YOU

Satan peeked in my future and saw what God had in store for me and sent the enemy to try and destroy me. The thief cometh not, but for to steal, and to kill, and to destroy: I am come that they might have life, and that they might have it more abundantly. John 10:10

Sixty days of pain and sixty days of anxiety with depression so bad I could not move or talk. I considered taking my life, felt isolated and vulnerable, scared to be, scared to live, in constant pain from my head to my feet, pains in my head, pulse racing, heart constantly pounding and couldn't close my eyes to sleep with the overload of mental anxiety. I could not compress my thoughts, but I still got up in the morning to begin my day with gratitude, maintained my normal routine with the kids and still made love to my husband. I fought to live and stayed in my prayer closet, sometimes falling asleep on the floor after asking God to cover me with His grace and heal my entirety. My prayer closet became my sanctuary. It is a small space but enough space for me to pray and cover my wall with hand written prayers. I would meditate and pray and fall asleep. The best sleep of my life. A peaceful sleep.

God held me and He kept me. He protected me from what was meant to destroy me. My God. Hallelujah. I kept thinking to myself, "If I can just make it to the other side and make it through this. God please don't take your hands off of my life. God please go before me and make a way.

I knew something was happening in my life. Weeks before November 30th, it felt like a transition was about to take place. Things were happening and people were being uprooted and removed from my life, but God protected me mentally, physically and emotionally. He gave me visions of what was about to happen. My spirit knew. At the time, I was a stay at home mom and wife raising three kids taking care of our family and household as well as everything else that comes along with being a mother and wife.

God kept giving me visions. I saw myself speaking, talking to people, large audiences and just doing what I love the most. My husband recently asked me what I was passionate about, and with all of the confidence in the world I said, "Talking!" This was after November 30th. I wasn't confident enough to share my truth to myself or him before then. But the truth is I love to talk. I love to talk to people and it is a gift from God. I love to counsel people. I love to share the love of God with people.

During those sixty days, it hurt to smile. I had to pray to God for His grace in the morning to get out of bed and take the kids to school. All of my life I have smiled and had a twinkle in my eye. My soul has always been filled with sunshine and morning remains my favorite part of the day. Waking up singing, "Goooood morningggggg, rise and shine; thank you God for this day."

ASK AND YE SHALL RECEIVE

I prayed and asked God to go before me and make a way. I prayed to God that he would send me to the right doctors. I asked God to choose my therapists and to send me angels that could help me understand what I was going through. I needed them to know how I got through it. I asked God to order my steps and He did. I met some of the most amazing doctors. During my very first appointment with the primary physician, she hugged and cried with me explaining she knew how I felt because it happened to her. She was an Angel. She talked with me, rubbed my back, gave me great advice, and just soothed my nerves and let me know I was going to be okay – and then she prayed with me.

I had a visit with my OB-GYN and her first words to me were, "you are not crazy," but trust me I felt crazy after she said that and she proceeded to recommend anti-depressants and a psychologist. You have to advocate for yourself. Even when there is doubt from your doctor, keep asking questions and seeking alternatives. You know your body and you can feel when something is not right. I begged my OB-GYN to test my hormones several times and she repeatedly said they were normal. I visited a specialist and found that I had an hormone imbalance. I begin to research hormonal changes, perimenopause and menopause symptoms, western and eastern medication. Make it a habit to be your number one supporter and advocate.

GIVE IT TO GOD

Living with so much stress, pressure, anxiety, depression and debilitating pain and still having to get up can be unsettling. The most consistent thing in my life was talking to God asking for covering and healing; praising Him; thanking God for my life; my children; my family; the sun; our home; His grace and mercy. Through the pain I thanked God. Gratitude is healing. Gratitude is a gateway to God.

When I couldn't talk, I moaned. My mom told me to keep moaning because that was the Holy Spirit. I worshiped Him through the pain, anxiety, and doubt. I surrendered to God.

YOU CANNOT MAKE IT WITHOUT GOD IN YOUR LIFE

I laid my burdens at His feet. Each day felt worse but I prayed and thanked God anyway. Sunday's were the best for me. I would look forward to church service online and tithing. I spent time reflecting on the message and the goodness of God's grace every second every hour of the day.

INTERLUDE

ACTION WORDS

THERE ARE WORDS THAT I BELIEVE WILL ACTIVATE THE HOLY SPIRIT

Sometimes you can only mumble because you are in so much pain and disarray. Sometimes you are crying so hard, so depressed, so low you cannot even pray for yourself. When life is heavy and your spirit is under attack, mumble, scream, whisper these words when you can't even find the words to talk to God:

HELP ME LORD
HALLELUJAH
THANK YOU LORD
DELIVER ME
GLORY GLORY
IT'S ME, GOD
I NEED HELP
I'M FIGHTING, GOD
I SURRENDER TO YOU
JESUS JESUS
GOD HELP ME
JEHOVAH JIREH
MY GOD
FILL ME WITH YOUR SPIRIT
GLORY TO GOD
YOUR GRACE AND MERCY

HOLY SPIRIT

LORD, HAVE MERCY

HOLDING ON TO YOUR GARMENT

HELP ME LORD

COVER ME GOD

THIS TOO SHALL PASS

GOD I MUST LIVE AND NOT DIE

GOD GO BEFORE ME AND MAKE A WAY

I PRAISE YOU LORD

I TRUST YOU LORD

I BELIEVE GOD

I'M THANKFUL

I'M DELIVERED

THANK YOU FATHER GOD

I'M STANDING IN THE NEED OF PRAYER

HEAL ME

REPLENISH ME

SAVE ME

I MAGNIFY YOUR NAME

MAY YOUR WILL BE DONE

BLESS THE NAME OF JESUS

GOD, SAVE ME FROM MYSELF

9. OWNING MY TRUTH

GIVE YOURSELF GRACE

Better yet, receive the grace that is already available to you each morning. Take a deep breath. Inhale. Exhale. It's okay. Life is okay. You are okay. Begin with the first step and God will guide the rest. It takes effort, but you will heal. You will begin again. You are alive. You are well. Close your eyes and imagine yourself in your destiny. Dream about your future self. Get excited and ready to meet your future self. Embrace your future self. Get ready to walk in your full purpose filled with peace, love, faith, compassion, family, fun, Gods' grace and His mercy. Hallelujah!

THE DEVIL IS A LIE

Anxiety will have you thinking you don't deserve to be happy daily and that is a lie. You can be happy every single day of your life. Anxiety will have you thinking about the end:the end of life and the end of the day instead of allowing life to play out, your mind has already fast-forwarded to the end – and that is a lie. You do not have to think about death every day of your life. Death does not have to consume your thoughts, or your life. Many times I have been laughing and having a great time, then in a split second ANXIETY appears and my mind automatically shifts to the negative. And it is a lie..

SUFFERING IN SILENCE

Whew, where do I start? The beginning of 2022 I was still having anxiety attacks every day. It felt as if my mind did not belong to me. Every day I was fighting for peace of mind – a mind that isn't running in a million different directions at the same time. One thing about anxiety is it opens up your mind to reflect and wonder how it arrived? As that thought process begins, the journey of reflecting unfolds and reveals the untold. What are my triggers? How often am I having anxiety attacks? What happens throughout the day? It's a hard conversation to have, but it is necessary to begin your journey of living an anxiety-free life. God is with you.

THE OTHER SIDE

I made it. I made it to the other side. Hallelujah. Old skin shed to begin Anew. The healing is in your journey, processing each day to make sure your tomorrow is better than your yesterday. I felt a release when I sat in my mess. I didn't deny or try to run from the truth that I was depressed and having anxiety. I wanted to understand the "why" I wanted to find the root of it so I could find my way to healing. I stopped worrying about how many days I had anxiety and focused on how I would be able to live my life with no anxiety. There's no set amount of days or hours. Focus on God every day and begin to imagine the life you desire and for me that was a life of no anxiety and depression. I prayed for a peaceful and sound mind and as the journey continued each day the pain would get lighter and lighter then there was peace. My mind and thoughts were clear and I could begin anew. But the work does not stop, it becomes a part of your daily routine of making sure you have a healthy mind and you are spiritually connected to God. Constantly feeding your mind healthy thoughts and images and giving yourself space and grace. We all deserve it.

SPIRITUALLY GIFTED

I have always been blessed with spiritual gifts and understood them at a young age due to my mom. I have always had visions. When I meet someone, I meet their spirit, not their flesh. I speak to the spirit. People can look absolutely stunning on the outside and full of dust on the inside. Don't let the flesh fool you. Always speak in the spirit. Ask God to show you His ways and anoint your spirit to see others.

THE MASTER'S PLAN

God has a plan for your life. You are enough. You are worthy. Your goals, admirations are not too much. They are not enough. God wants us to enjoy life. He wants us to be the best version of ourselves. He has the master plan for our lives and it includes more than we could ever imagine. Just think about this -everything you are thinking about that you want or desire out of life is not even close to what God wants for your life. Focus on the more. Wake up with gratitude in your heart. Tell God your desires in life. And it's not always about material things. Dwell on the spiritual things you desire in life - a fulfilling relationship with Christ, His peace and mercy over your life and Agape love to see your life through God's eyes.

MY SAVING GRACE

Talk to Him. God is my everything. As much as I love my husband, he is not my everything. God is the head of my life and because of my relationship with Him, I am able to have beautiful, healthy relationships with the ones I love. I am able to love my husband and my family because of the way Christ loves me. Because God is the head of my life, I talk to God before I talk to my husband. I always ask God to go before me and make a way, guide my heart and my words. When I communicate with my husband, he is able to receive what I am saying to him because God has already put it on his heart and in his spirit.

I can't even tell you how many times I talk to God in a day. It is literally all day – He is in my thoughts and my spirit. You can never get enough time talking with God. He is always listening and there for us. I am constantly in a praying state of mind and heart of gratitude throughout the day. When I am walking, talking, driving, sitting, as long as I am breathing I am talking to God. I walk by people and I pray for them. A smile and a prayer goes a long way. Talking to God is a part of my life. I am in constant communication with God.

I could not have made it without Him. Each step I took to get to a better place was His grace in my life. I owe it all to Him. And if you ever ask how I made it, I will tell you God did it and God will do the same for you.

A PRAYER FOR YOU

Father God, I come to you, Lord, with a bowed head and a humble heart thanking you for this day; your day; a new day. Hallelujah Holy God.Thank you for blessing me to open my eyes and place my feet on solid ground. Thank you God for blessing me to rest well and wake well. Thank you God for covering me with your peace and protecting me from any hurt, harm or danger. Thank you for your grace, mercy, and love. Thank you for my life. Thank you God for choosing me to be here to be alive and well. God, forgive me of my sins. Forgive me, O Lord, for anything that I have said and done that has been against your will. Thank you, Heavenly Father, for protecting my family today, yesterday and always. Thank you God for your peace, your prosperity, your covering. God, you are my everything. With you God all things are possible. Thank you God for the comfort of our home, warm beds, food and clothing. Thank you God for the laughter and warmness that fills our home. God, I ask that you cancel any and all weapons formed against me that they will not prosper. God, please protect me from what is meant to cause me harm. God, please go before me and make a way. Please guide my heart and my words and order my steps. Be the lamp to my feet God and a light to my path. Bless me, O Lord, that my God-given light may shine so bright that when people see me, they may know that Christ Jesus dwells in me. Thank you, Father. I love and I honor you. Please keep my mind, my heart, my spirit on You God. No more of me God all of you. Speak through me. Jesus, guide my words and my heart. God give me strength to carry on. God, I plead the blood of Jesus over my family. No weapon formed against us shall prosper. God, please go before my family and make a way. Guide our hearts and order our steps. Bless us Lord that we may do your will. Have your way with us, God. Bless us Lord that we may be still and hear your voice. God, I cancel all anxiety, fear, worry and panic. Wrap your loving arms around this world God heal us where we are broken. God, I cancel anything that is not of You. Father God, we praise and magnify your name. In Jesus' Holy and Divine Name we pray we thank you God. Amen.

HOPEFUL LIFE

Hope is the key to life. Hope is believing you are already in a better place. Hope is believing you are already healed. Hope is knowing you will make it to the other side. Hope is believing God will deliver you from your pain. Hope is trusting God. Hope is having faith in something you cannot see, but can feel. Hope is praising God through the storm. Hope is walking in your purpose. Hope is laying your burdens at the feet of God. Hope is love. Hope is beautiful.

How do you eliminate anxiousness? How do you make it go away for good? How do you slow down a racing mind? How do you stop the agonizing pain in your brain from constant overthinking? With God. This is the answer to your prayers. This is the answer to your pain. God is your source of relief. God is your healer. Trust and obey Him. God is looking for a deeper relationship with you.

A PRAYING MOTHER

My mother and I have always had a close relationship. It's a friendship that goes deeper than friends. I must say, we have a spiritual bond. From the age of 13, I realized if I just listen to my mother and do what I am supposed to do, I can see her beautiful smile and not hear her fuss at me or put me on punishment. I started to really listen to the advice she was pouring into me about life, relationships, God, family, school and friends, and it all really began to make sense. I applied her God given advice to my life, and it felt like I was always two steps in front of a potential disaster because I was able to make wise decisions. In high school, she became my confidant. We talked about everything and she always gave the best advice . It was a spiritual connection. She poured the love of Christ into me and taught me to accept Jesus Christ as my Lord and Savior and friend at a very early age. I learned to talk to Him, lean on Him and trust Him. God became my everything.

I was a miracle baby for my parents. As a young married couple, they could not conceive. I remember my mom telling me how her and my dad got on their knees and prayed specifically for me. They changed their life, and nine months later after a healthy, happy pregnancy, here comes a healthy and happy baby - me! At a very young age, my mom understood I had spiritual gifts. I could see things most kids could not see. Around the age of 3 or 4 years old, I told my mom the kids were in the water. If you were alive during the unfortunate and horrific Atlanta child murders, then you would know exactly what I am talking about. Kids were being kidnapped, kids were not making it home from school, Black kids specifically.

She taught me to accept my gifts and poured so much confidence and humility into me. It became a badge of honor for me. Always smiling, always happy, always caring, loving, always present – my mother taught me the truth about life: the good, the bad and the ugly. She did not sugar coat anything when it came to the truth. She always gave true hard to hear advice with such love and grace. The same way she poured into me and nurtured my spirit, still to this day, she does with her granddaughters and grandson. I can still feel my mother's prayers. I can feel her spirit today. I love the way we love, laugh and the way we cover each other in prayer. I am beyond blessed and entirely grateful to live this life with her. Don't be afraid to talk to your kids about life and about God. You will calm their imagination by giving them truthful thoughts and open the door for healthy dialogue. If you see spiritual gifts in your children, make sure they embrace them, let them know it is nothing to be afraid of and their gifts come from God.

INVISIBLE

I was invisible to my own family. Invisible to my husband. Invisible to my kids. They expected me to be present, and readily available. Always a yes from me. Take the kids to school, and if they need or forgot something at home, I'm running it back. Not to mention - going to the grocery store, cooking dinner, cleaning the house, laundry, soccer practice, track practice, events on the weekend and whatever and whenever my husband wanted or needed something, he got it. I was doing everything for them and nothing for myself. I was completely and utterly burned out and didn't even know it. Their tanks were full while my tank was empty. My family had everything at their fingertips. Whatever they wanted, they would get from me, but at what cost? I did not have a moment for myself and I needed a moment to just breathe. But could I really be mad at them? I created this environment for them.

In my journey of healing, I've learned a no to them is a yes for me. Saying no to my kids, my husband, or anyone but God, is a yes for me and reassures me that I am putting myself first.

GOD GO BEFORE ME AND MAKE A WAY

If you write down anything from this book, this is your time to put pen to paper.

"God, go before me and make a way."

This is my daily mantra. I say this repeatedly throughout my day. Asking God to go before me and make a way is asking God to cover every aspect of my life. It is a prayer of protection and a prayer of surrendering to God that my life will be led by HIM. I am asking God to order my steps. Asking God to enter life before I do is the best feeling in life.

I pray this over my husband, my children, my family, friends and myself. These words have saved my life. There is power in these words. Say this every day. Start your day with these words, God go before me and make a way. God, order my steps. Carry these words with you; they are life changing.

10. LIVING ANXIETY FREE

My first step to an anxiety free life was to calm my mind with overthinking. I prayed to God specifically to calm my mind and thoughts; bless me with a sound and healthy mind. My thoughts would get the best of me anticipating a day that had not even occurred. When you realize that God is the only One already in the days ahead, you welcome the calmness of His presence in your life. Anxiety, fear and worry are not of God, and because of my relationship with Christ, I fight every single day of my life to rid what is not of Him. My mom would always say to me growing up, "Shari, how do you eat an elephant? One bite at a time." This African proverb is so true to life. One day at a time. One step at a time. Do not get overwhelmed in your own thoughts. Breathe through each moment. And when you are overwhelmed give to God and enjoy your day.

FALL BACK

Have you ever closed your eyes and leaned back into the arms of the person behind you? Scary, right? But there is no fear leaning onto the One Who created you. Fall back into Christ. Fall back into His grace. Trust the plans God has for your life. Once you get in the game, God will give you the playbook. Self-doubt, worry, anxiety, fear do not own you and do not belong in your life. You can fight any battle with God. Trust that God will heal you and see you through this by taking the first step to the beginning of the rest of your life. It is time to find your light again.

Find what makes you happy. Your happiness may look different from what people expect from you and that is perfectly okay. This is your life. Live it.

LESSON PLANS

Or as my Mom says, God's Lessons Pans. God has a plan for your life. Your life has purpose. Each day you rise is a new day to live, and I mean LIVE. Do whatever makes you happy and brings you God's tranquility and peace. Live each day with grace and be intentional with your actions. One thing for sure, each day will not look the same. Some days you are mentally exhausted, and your mind and body both need rest. Know what that looks like and be prepared to pull out your arsenal of remedies.

- My personal remedies:
- Rest
- Talking to God
- Hydration
- Breathing through a straw (it works)
- Protecting my peace
- Prayer
- Meditation
- Tea time (I'm such a tea snob),
- Quietness
- Talking with my Mama
- Cleaning a clutter filled space in my home
- Exercise
- Daily walks
- Stretching
- Social media block
- Sitting in your emotions
- Writing how I feel

- Music
- Spa time
- Reading
- Relaxing
- Breathing exercises
- Sitting still
- Lunch with a friend

Find your remedies and be mindful of them.

I think about all the time I've wasted in life overthinking and talking myself out of living my best life. I spend time thinking I'm not good enough or qualified because of fear and anxiety. I am fearfully and wonderfully made. God made me with purpose. Greatness lives in me.

WHAT'S IN MY BAG?

If you know that an anxiety attack is near or could happen, be ready for it. Be prepared. I've learned to keep track of the anxiety attacks and it's triggers: stress, overthinking, menstrual cycle, overwhelmed. lack of communication with loves ones, unresolved issues, new environments, and I am still learning.

Take control over the anxiety. Make it powerless. In my bag, I have one thing with me at all times and it is called AnxioCalm. It's safe enough for a 4 year old and its main ingredient is echinacea. There are so many benefits to the popular herbal remedy echinacea. It is known to reduce anxiety, stress and nervous tension.

One day, my spirit led me to my local herb store, Herbal Planet. I walked in broken and in tears full of anxiety, wearing a mask only revealing my eyes. I met a kind woman named Laura. I asked her if she could show me what was good for anxiety. She saw the tears and just grabbed me, hugged me, and prayed with me. God will always send you an Angel. I began to visit the herb store weekly. I became totally indulged in teas and what herbs could help me. I tried everything she suggested and it worked. Every morning and evening, I made time for tea. A cup of grace in a cup. I learned what worked for me with the help of Laura and the wonderful Herbal Planet staff. Tea time became my favorite time of the day. I looked forward to the sound of my tea kettle, the whistling of the pot was soothing to my soul, slicing fresh lemons, a fresh squeezed orange with pulp and the addition of local honey, cinnamon sticks, cloves, crystallized ginger along with cranberry powder and ashwagandha powder with my favorite tea bags. Whew! Healing in a cup. I loved that I created that time for me. The process of making tea became fulfilling and healing.

FAVORITE TEA RECIPES
All teas are caffeine free

A CUP OF GRACE
Mango Ginger Tea
Hibiscus Tea
Green Tea
Fresh squeezed lemon
Sliced Oranges
Local honey
Cranberry Powder
Cinnamon Stick
Crystallized Ginger

BE MY PEACE
Chamomile
Peppermint

Holy Basil
Local Honey
Cloves
Fresh squeezed lemon
Sliced Oranges
Local honey
Cranberry Powder
Cinnamon Stick
Crystallized Ginger

PAIN RELIEF
Red raspberry leaf
Cranberry Powder
Ashwagandha Powder
Fresh squeezed lemon
Sliced Oranges
Local honey
Cranberry Powder
Cinnamon Stick
Crystallized Ginger

HEALING
Turmeric
Moringa
Passion Flower

Peppermint
Lemongrass
Fresh squeezed lemon
Sliced Oranges
Local honey
Cranberry Powder
Cinnamon Stick
Crystallized Ginger

REST WELL, WAKE WELL
Chamomile
Peppermint
Cinnamon Stick

CONVERSATION WITH YOUR PAST

My Mom has always said that everything starts
from your childhood. As humans, we walk
around earth looking normal while we are
broken. We are broken from what we did not
heal from - trauma from our childhood, abuse
from relationships, unspoken family stories that
we carry to our graves. For better or worse, our
past can control our future. It does not matter
how successful you are as an adult, if you do not
heal from what hurt you in the past, it will

continue to break you internally and hurt your relationships and this can trigger anxiety.

Just imagine being on top of a mountain that you climbed and conquered. Cool breeze embraces your face as the sun shines on you. Just imagine the feeling of accomplishment and victory after reaching the mountain top. That is what forgiveness feels like. There's freedom in forgiveness and forgiveness is always for you. When you have God as your personal Savior, you are able to view forgiveness differently. Forgiveness allows your planted feet to move forward and away from hurt and pain. Forgive who has hurt you. Forgiving people who have hurt you gives you control of your life. It makes them powerless. They can no longer control the narrative. Take your power back.

There are people in my past that have hurt me, but just imagine if I waited and waited and waited for them to say, "Shari I am so sorry." What if I waited years to hear the words, I forgive you.

Why? Because God teaches us to forgive. The freedom you feel for yourself when you forgive the person(s) who hurt you is priceless and unmatched. You feel lighter when you let go and surrender to God. Forgive and begin to move forward with your life.

LIVING IN A SPACE OF GRATITUDE

What does living in a space of gratitude look like? What do I have to do to live in gratitude? God, I thank You! Yes, it is just that simple. Say thank You. Live with gratitude in your heart, gratitude in your mind, gratitude in your thoughts and gratitude in your actions. When you surround your life in gratitude, you drown out the anxiety. When I begin to feel anxious, I take slow deep breaths and immediately look around me and name things I am grateful for to God. This is soothing to me and brings me peace and comfort.

MY TRUTH

I fought to be here. Through the darkness, pain and uncertainty, my faith never wavered. God was with me. He held, healed, covered and protected me. I felt His presence in the moments I wanted to quit and give up. I felt His spirit with me. In my lowest moment, God was all I had. I surrendered my life to Him and told God to have His way. He saved me from myself. He calmed my mind and my thoughts. He made me better than I was before. I didn't know how or when my days would get better, but I trusted God for better days. And I am still thanking God this day for even better days. He is my rock and my salvation. I am eternally thankful.

I stand on the shoulders of my praying ancestors, my praying mother, my praying father, my praying family and tribe.

Through my pain I found my God-given purpose. I did not quit even when I wanted to quit and die. God held me and carried me through. I can do all things through Christ which strengthens me.

I never knew writing was in my future. I never thought I could be an author. It was never on my vision board. Though I am an avid reader, dreamer and love getting lost in a book, I never saw this for myself. I have traveled the world through the pages of a book. What has always been a part of my life, became my life. Through my pain I found my purpose. I am here. I am alive. I trust God. Thank you, God.

AFTERWORD

FREE

Everything I was searching for in life, I already had. God had already made a way for me. Everything I needed was already in my life. God just had to change my vision and now I see clearly. The peace I have within cannot be bought, but only given by God. My soul is different.

Thank you Jehovah Jireh. I am different. I talk differently. I walk differently. His grace fills me. His love carries me. His mercy saves me. His peace keeps me.

Father God, I pray for the person that is still searching to find you. Fill their heart with your love and grace. Bless them with your new mercies. Give them a new lens to see out of that they may see the vision you have for their life. Help them where they are hurting. Heal their soul God. I pray they search for your word, guidance and nurturing. May they find peace in talking with you. Fill their spirit with your goodness and grace. May they walk different. Talk different. Look different. Act different. Be their everything God.

Amen.

We are often searching for the material things as the prize, aren't we - the mansion, 12 cars and private island? What if we already have everything we need? God's peace and understanding; His grace; His love; His protection; our family; loved ones; joy; laughter; contentment; faith. When we prioritize what is important and show gratitude for what we have, the house, car and career will find you. May your heart be content. May you have a sound mind and clear thoughts. May you live the life God has for you with a heart of gratitude. May you laugh and dance. May you celebrate your victories in life. May you soar like an eagle. May your purpose find you. May you do what makes your soul happy. Not my ways but your ways, God. No more of me, God, all of you.

Made in the USA
Middletown, DE
23 January 2024

47966043R00064